Crocodile Tears

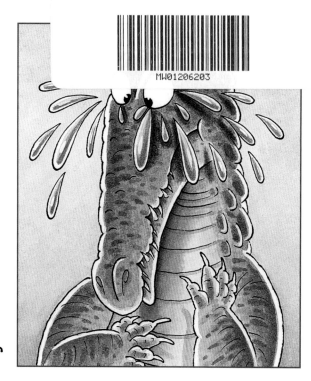

Poems by Jill Eggleton
Illustrated by Clive Taylor

CONTENTS

Crocodile Tears

"I have no friends,"
the crocodile cried.
"My friends have
gone away.

"I have no friends,"
the crocodile cried.
"I ate them all today!"

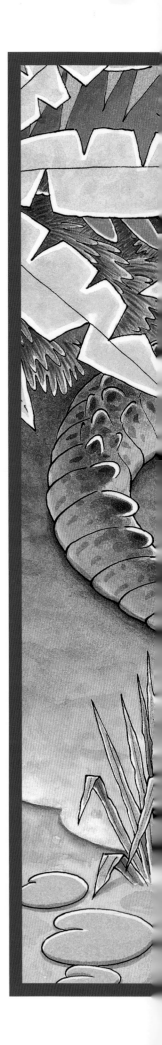

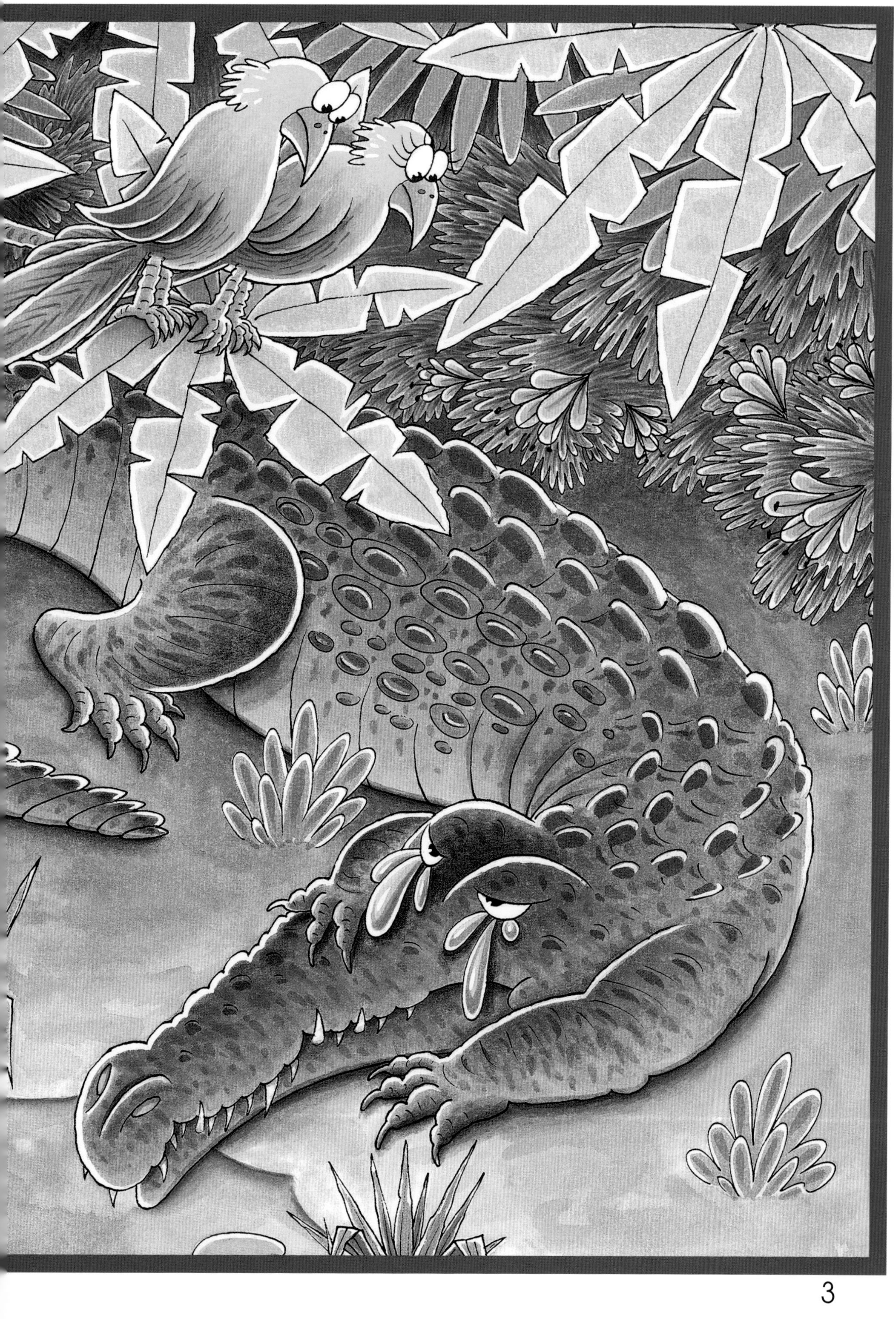

Ouch! Ouch! Ouch!

Mother Kangaroo
went . . .

jump, *jump,* jump!

Baby Kangaroo
went . . .

bump, *bump,* bump!

"Ouch!"
said the baby.
"Ouch! Ouch! Ouch!

"I don't like **bumping**
in this pouch!"

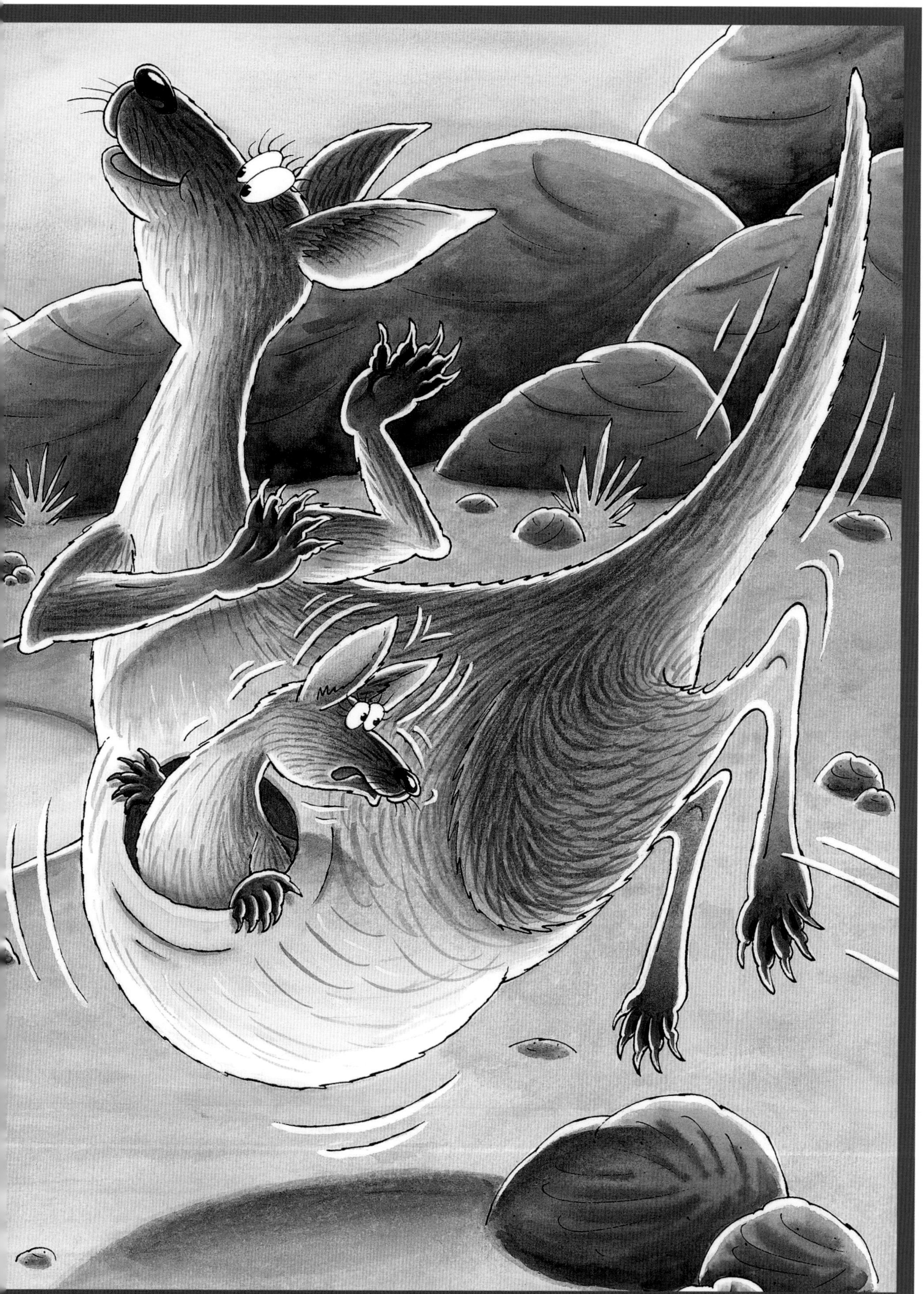

Cheese, Please

I don't want fish
to eat, eat, eat!

I don't want apples
and I don't want meat!

I don't want spinach
and I don't want peas!

I am a mouse,
and I want cheese!

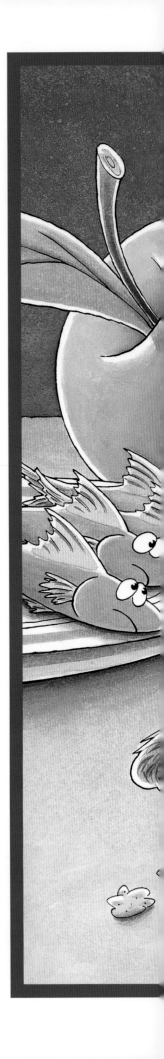

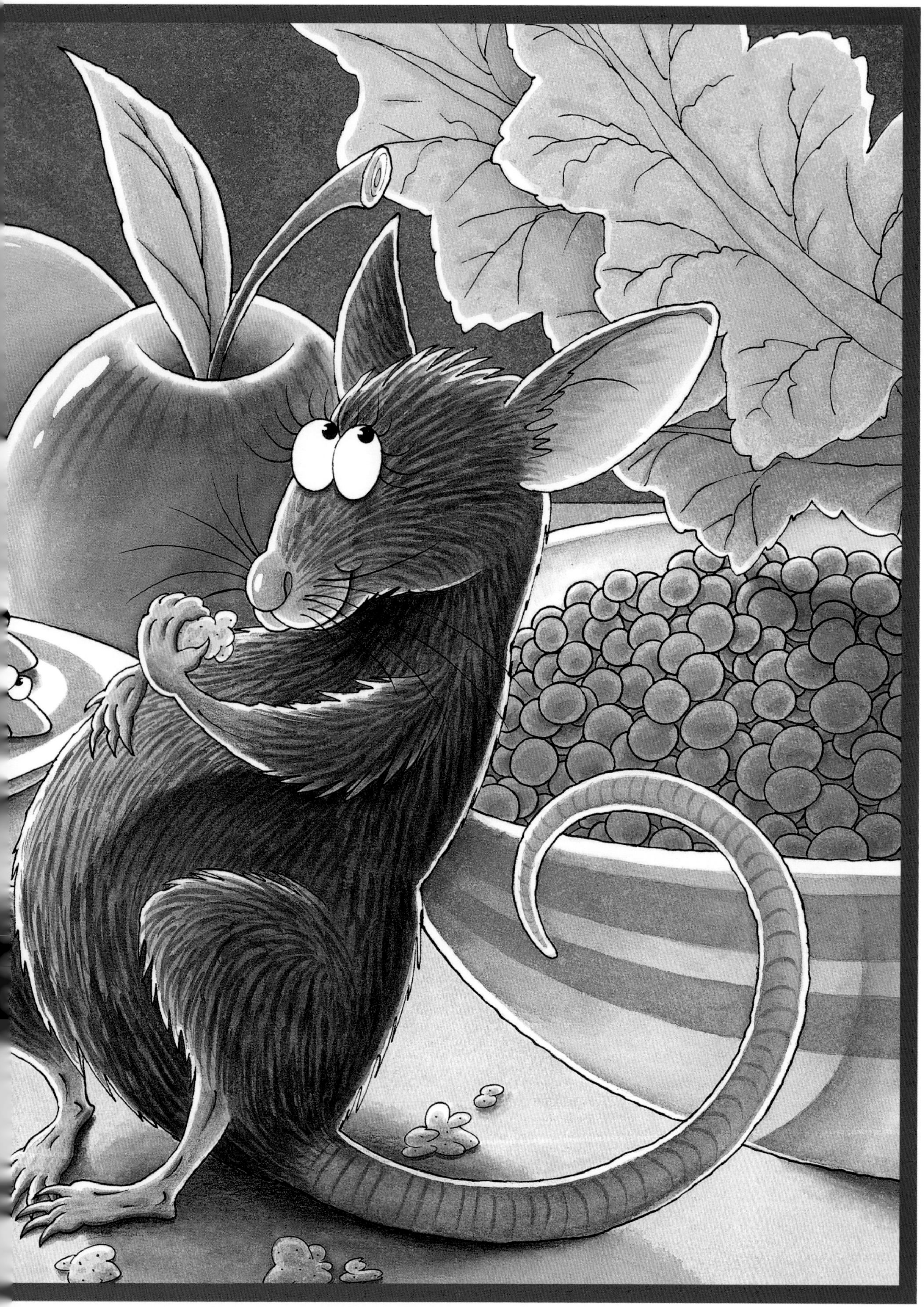

Hippo

The hippo said,
"Just look at me!
I am only gray."
So he sat
and he sat
and he sat —
he sat
in the sun all day.

"**Now** look at me,"
the hippo said.
"Tell me what you think!
I'm not gray,"
the hippo said,
"I'm not gray,
I'm pink!"

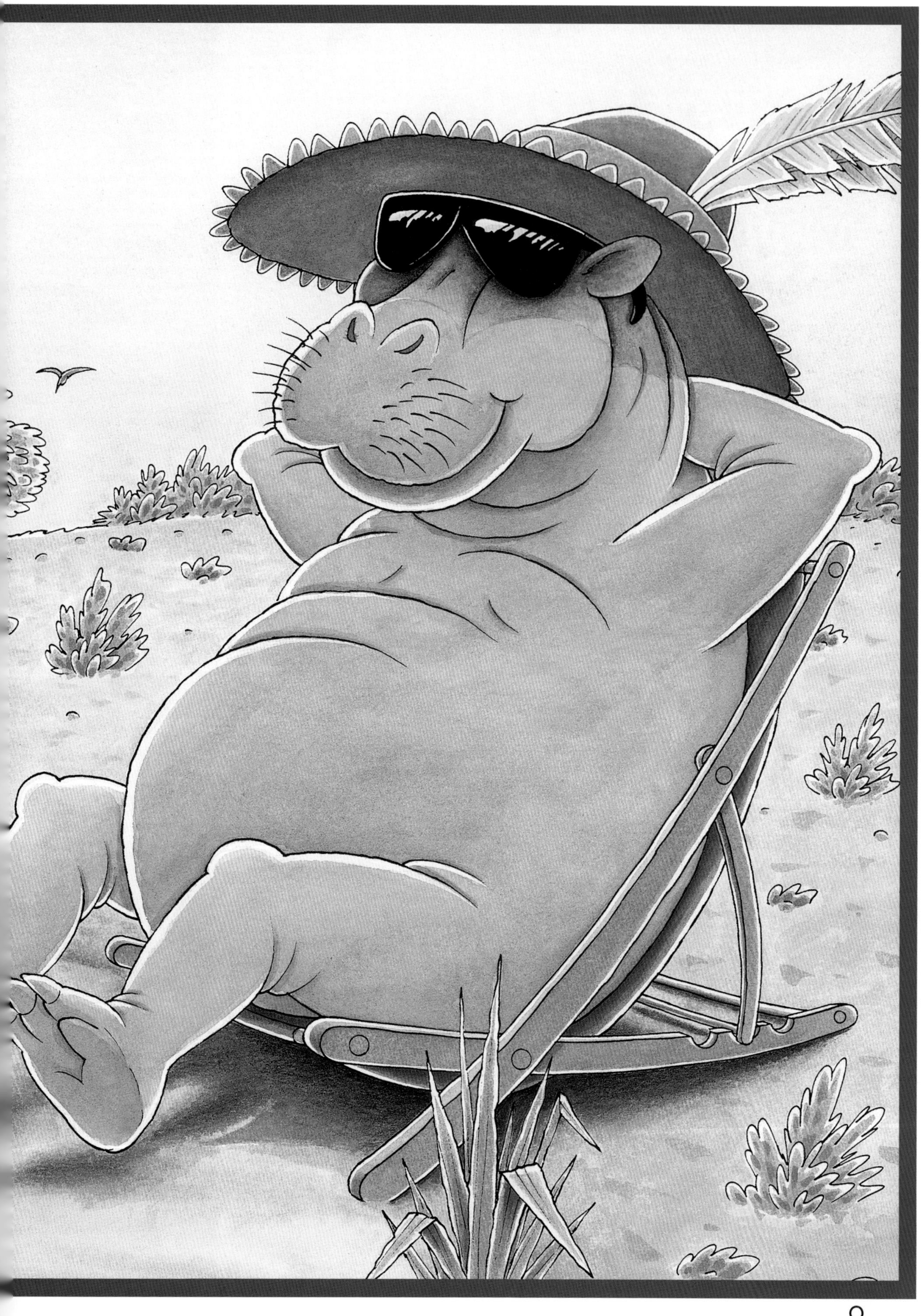

Mouse Measles

"Mouse has the
measles," Tiger said.

"He has spots on his back

and **spots** on his head.

He has spots on his tail

and **spots** on his toes,

and spots all over
his little mouse nose!"

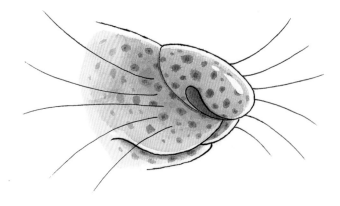

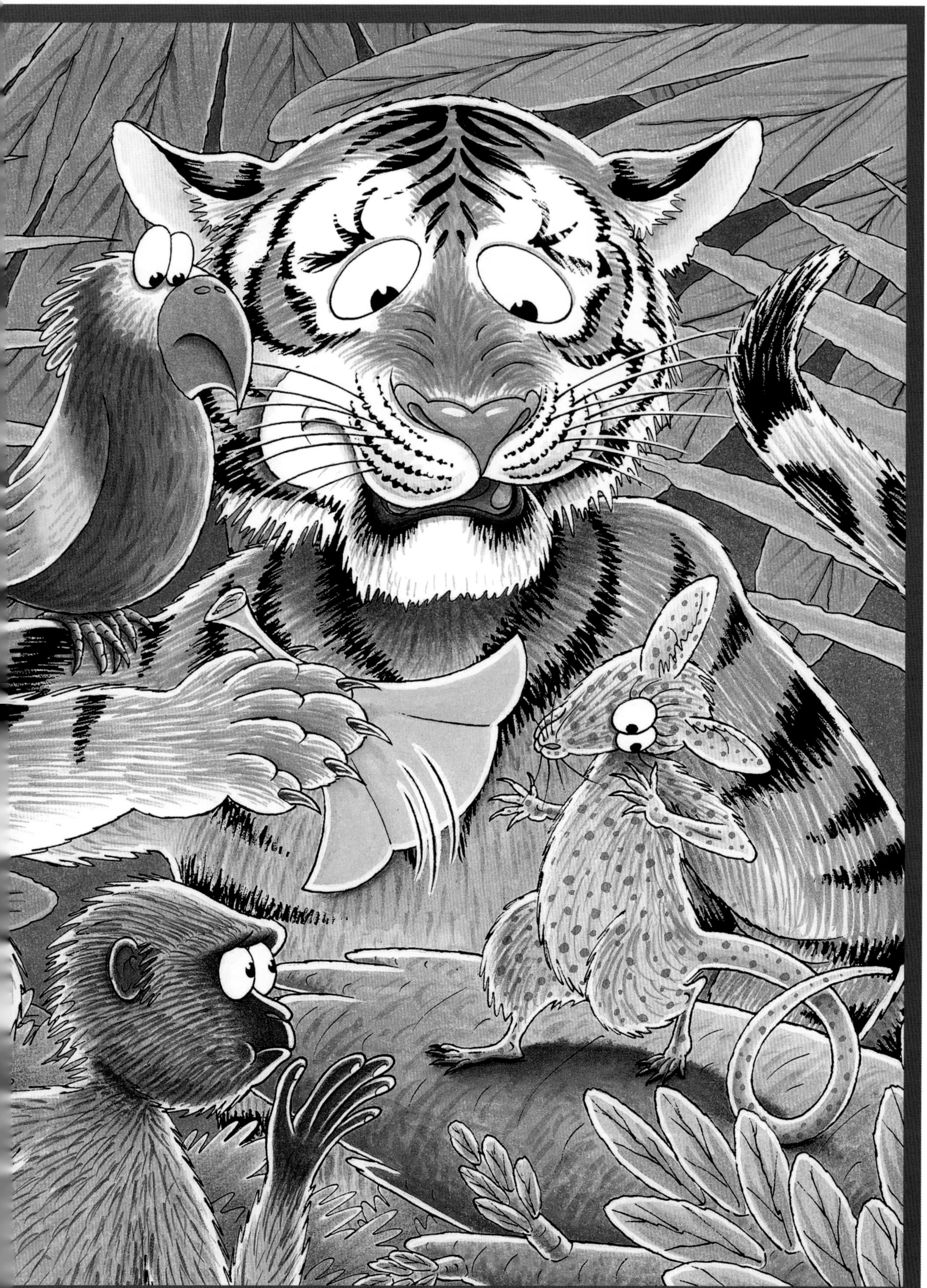

Camel

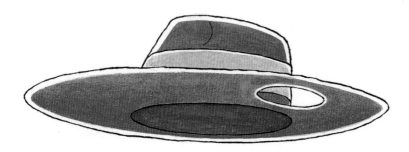

Camel got a sun hat.
It was a lovely red.
Now she has a hat
for her camel head!

Camel got a sun hat.
It was a lovely blue.
Now she has a hat
for her big hump, too!

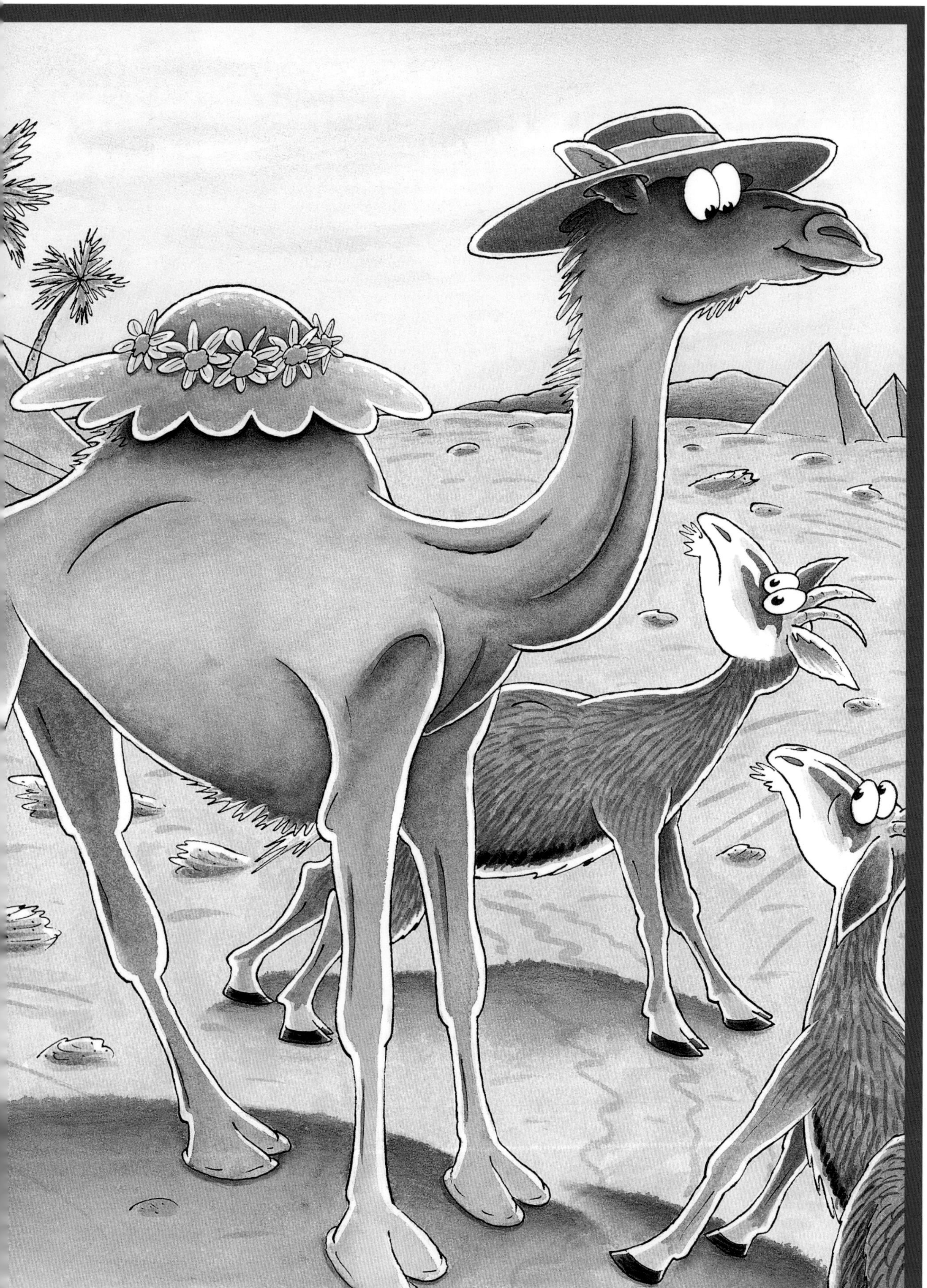

The Elephant's Trunk

The elephant has
a trunk,
like a *wiggly wiggly* hose.

The elephant has
a trunk,
but he hasn't got a nose!

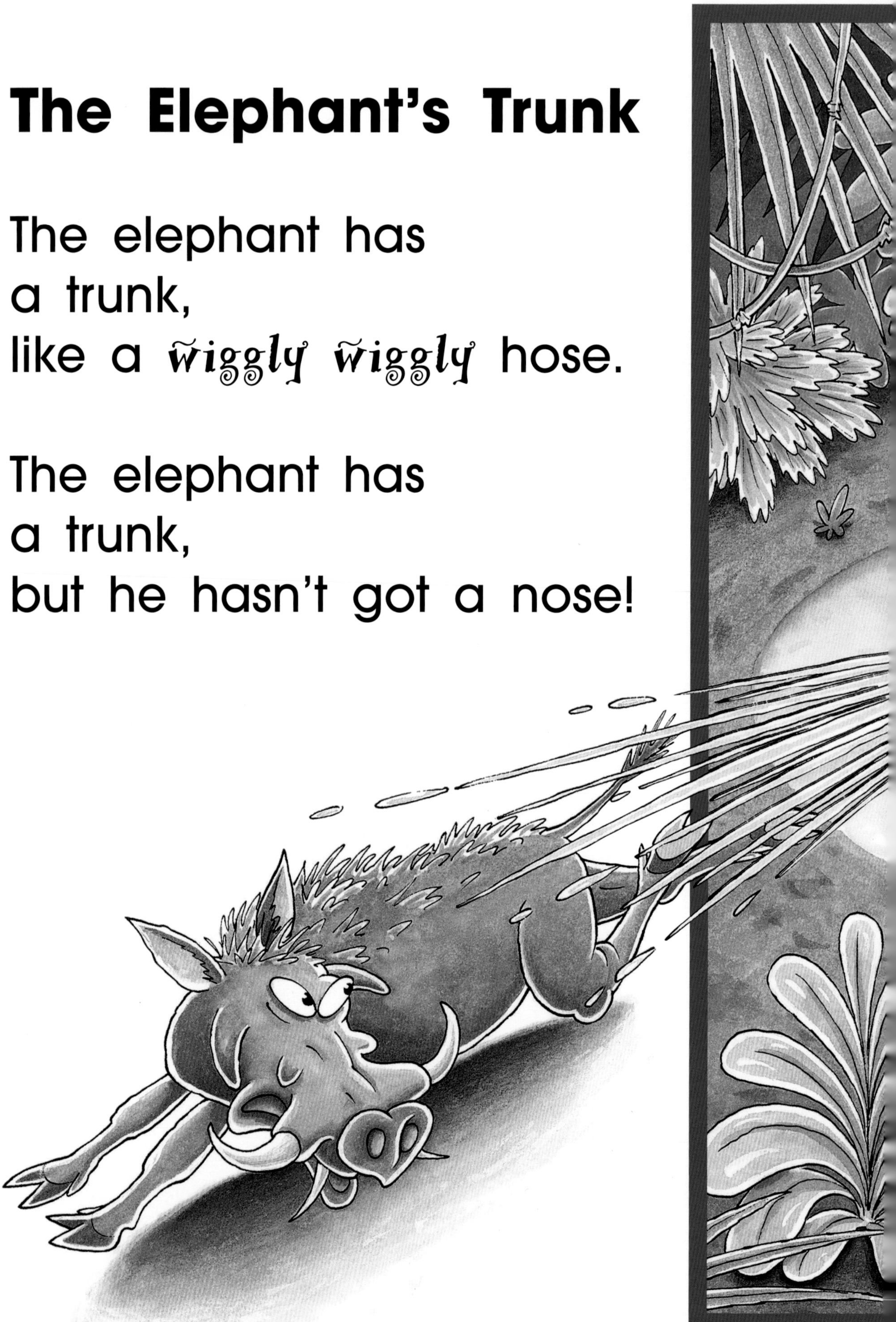

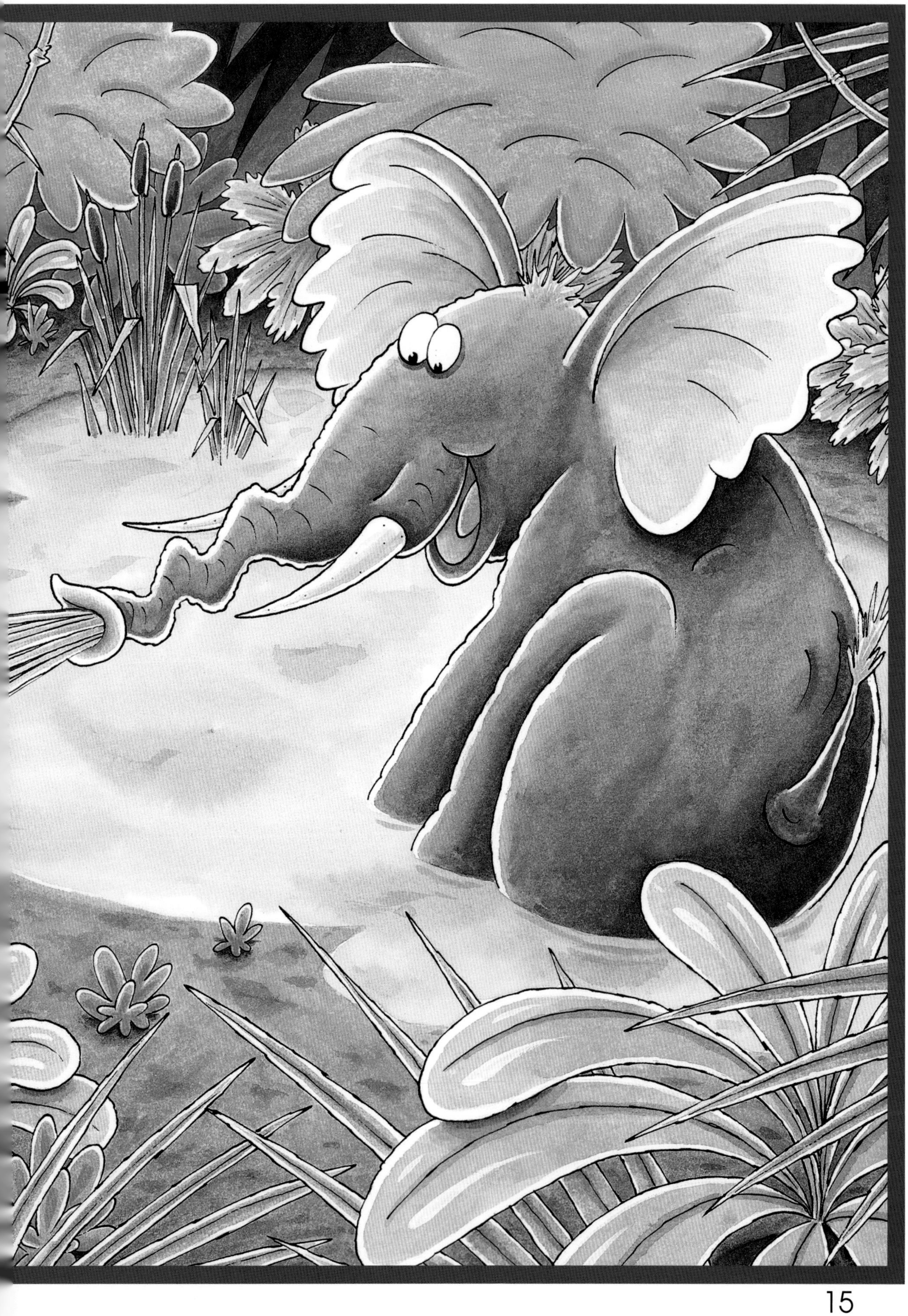

Look at the Snake!

Look at the snake!
Look at him crawl —
up the rock
and over the wall!

up the rock
and over the wall —
doesn't he hurt
his tummy at all?

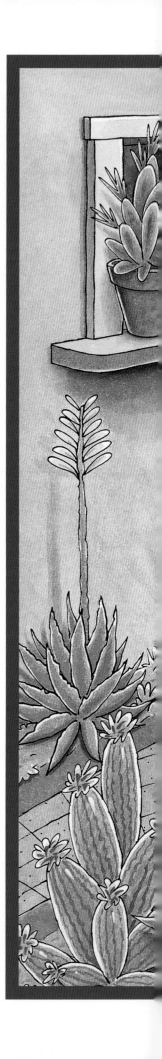

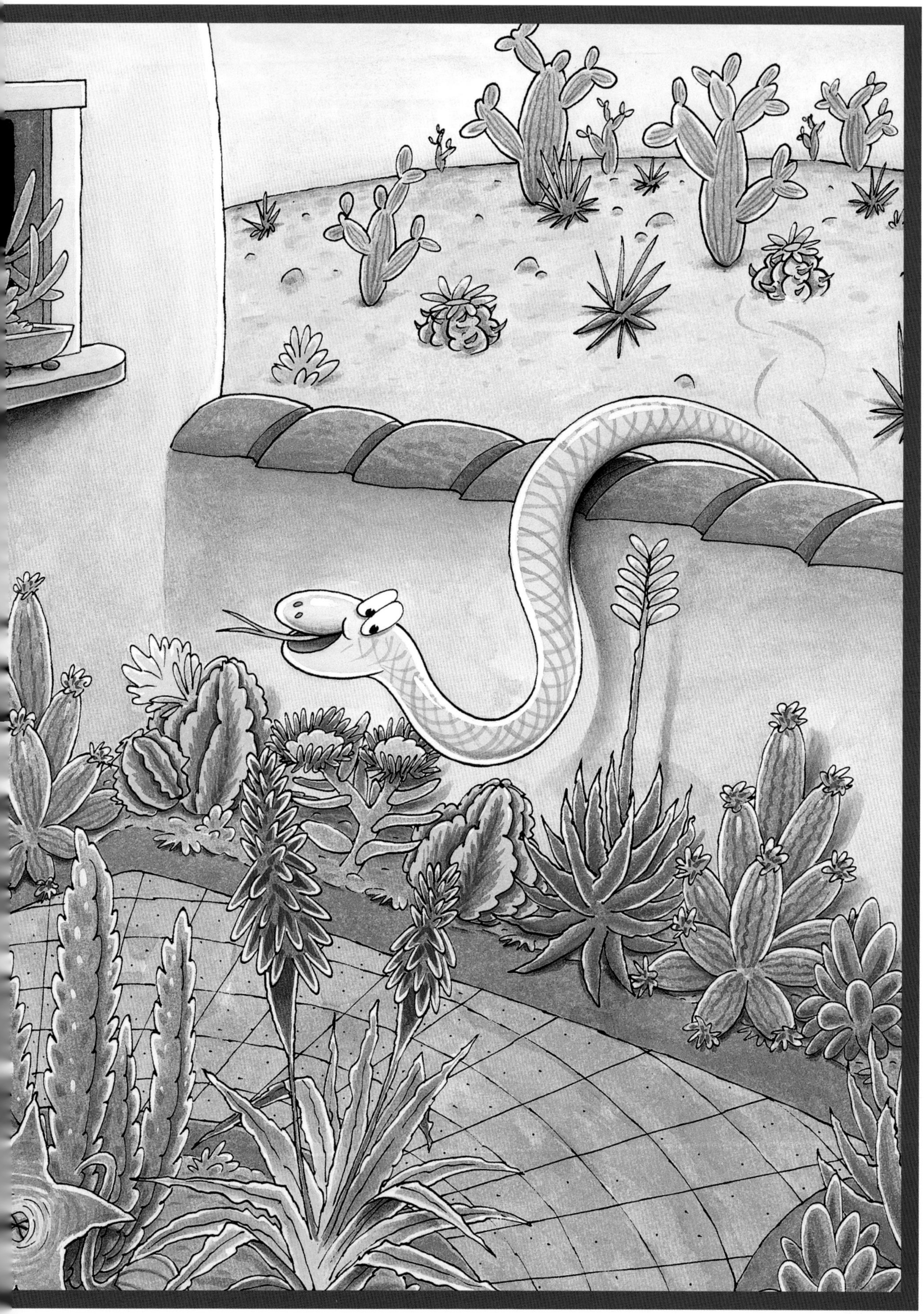

Centipede Dance

The centipede did
the centipede dance
up and down
the street.

The centipede had
centipede socks
on his funny feet.

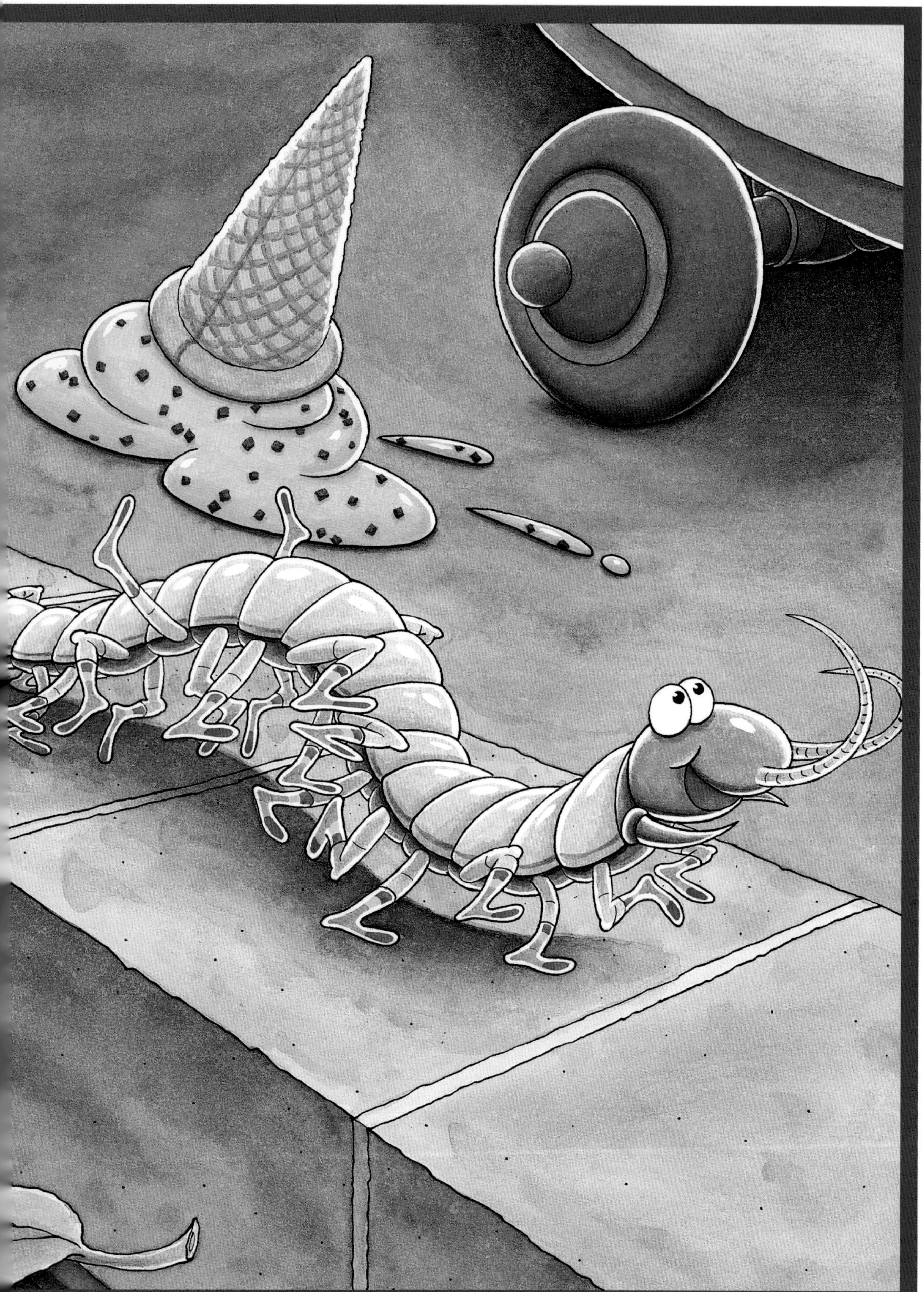

A Bird Came in My Window

A bird came in
my window

and hopped

along my bed.

And then it laid
a spotty egg,

ker-plonk

right on my head!

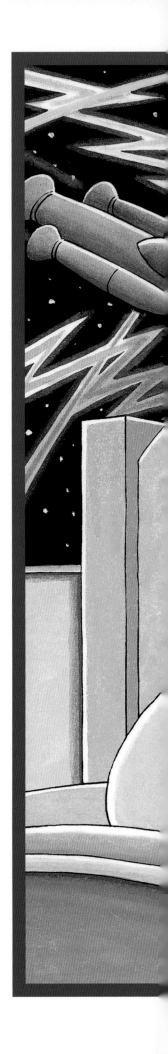

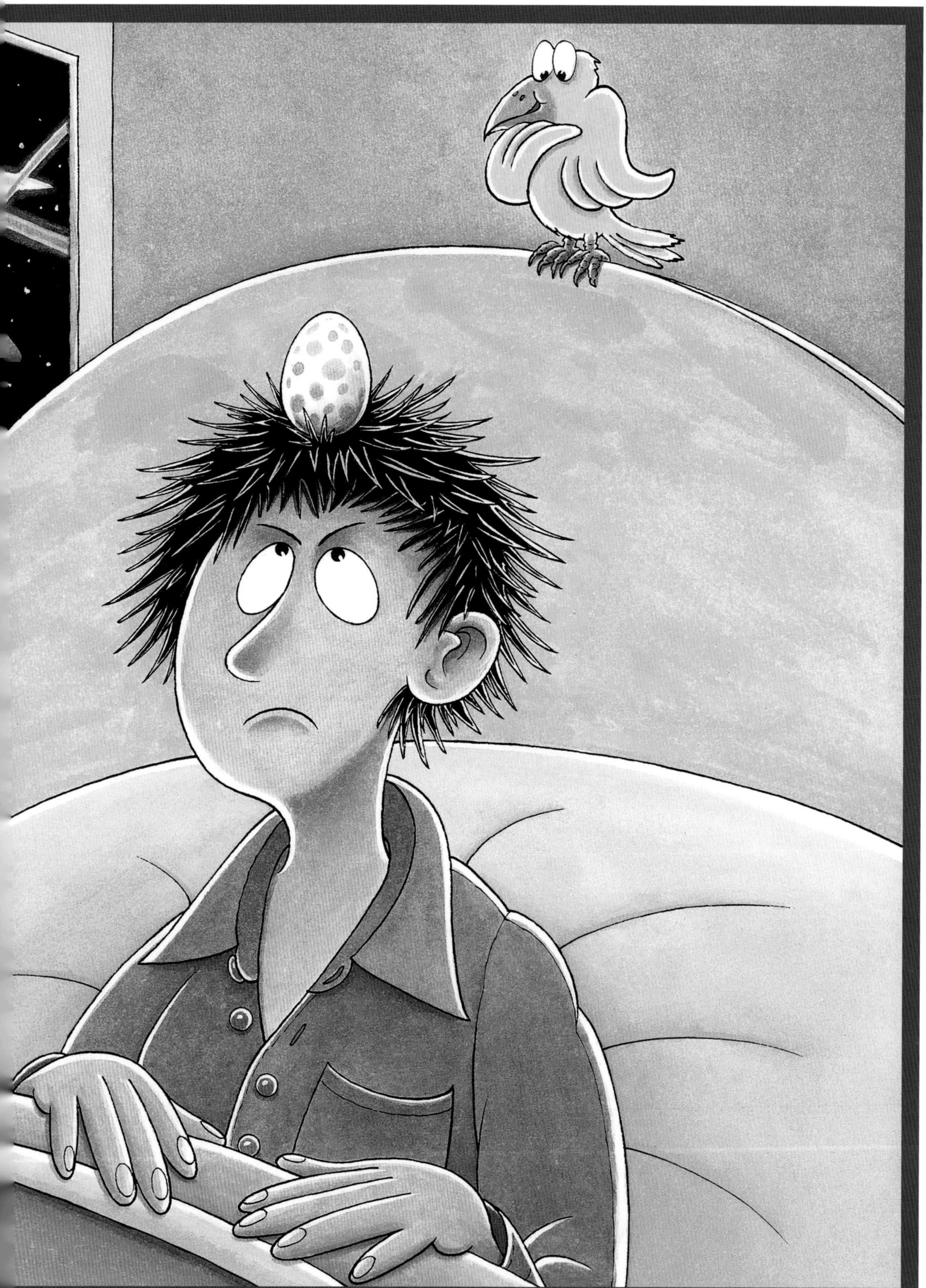

White Bear

White Bear,
White Bear,
where do you go
when you go walking
over the snow?

White Bear,
White Bear,
I can see
that you need boots
to wear like me!

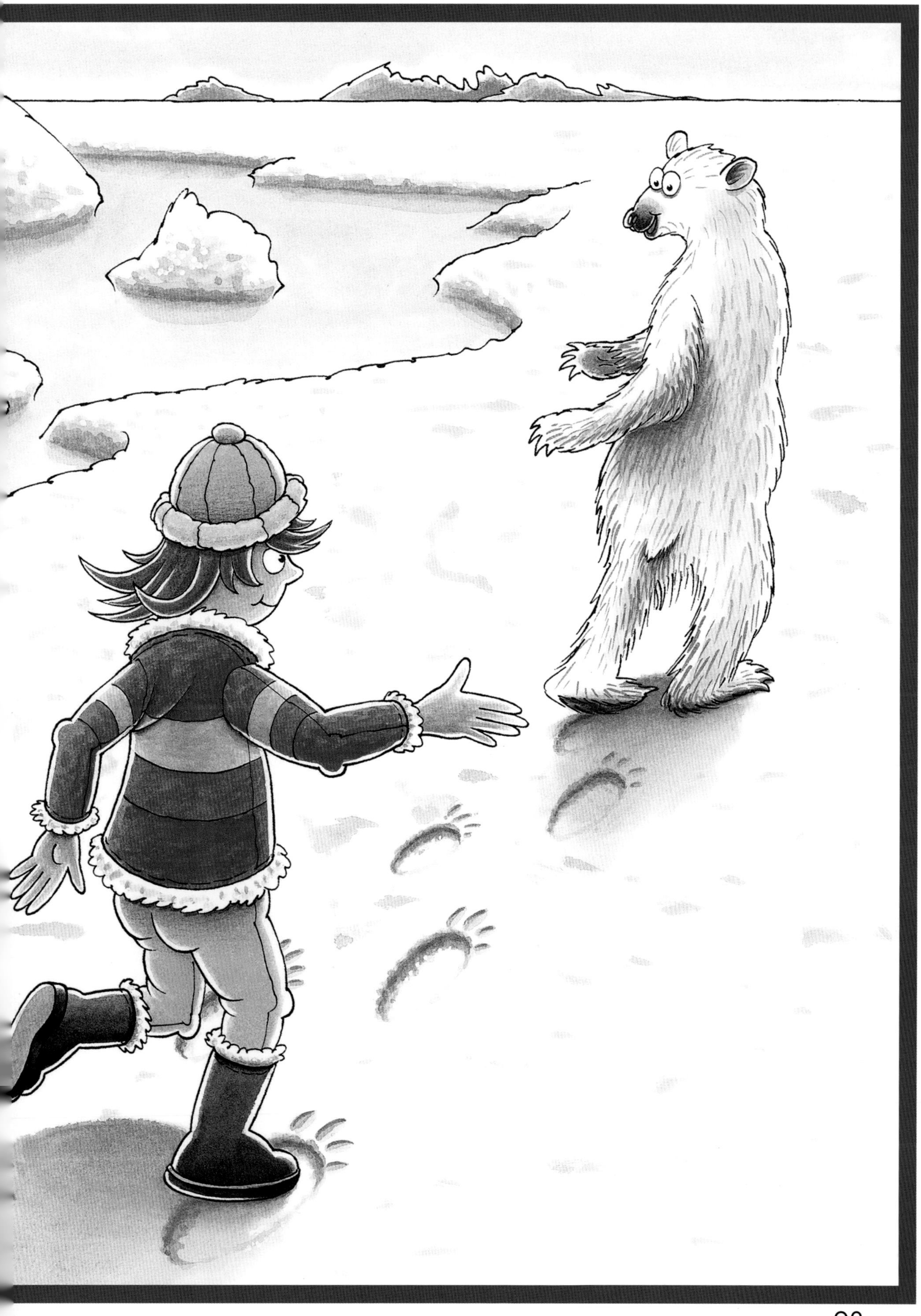

Excuse Me, Please

Mr. Giraffe,
you are
too tall.
You bumped
a nest
and made it fall!

When you go
walking under trees,
you should say,
"Excuse me, please!"